Remember to Feed the Kittens

Large Type Edition

A KERNEL BOOK
published by
NATIONAL FEDERATION OF THE BLIND

TABLE OF CONTENTS

Marc Maurer, President
National Federation of the Blind

EDITOR'S INTRODUCTION

This is the sixteenth Kernel Book. When we started the Kernel Book series some eight years ago we had little idea what a significant factor these little books would become in our work to change what it means to be blind. With more than three and a quarter million of them in circulation, it is fair to say that the way vast numbers of people think about blindness and blind people is different today from what it was before the Kernel Books.

And this, of course, is just what we wanted to accomplish. By sharing the stories of our lives with you—our fears and our failures, our hopes and our accomplishments—we want you to come to know us as real people. People you might meet in church, on the job, or in school.

We know that blindness can seem strange and even a little bit scary. We know that people who see us are sometimes curious and would like to be friendly, but often don't know what to say or how to start.

How does a blind teen-ager in love behave? What does a blind widow do when her teen-agers are ready to learn to drive? And, what about the blind college student who is told she must major in music? These are real-life happenings to real people—to us, the blind men and women you will meet in this book. We are happy to tell you our stories. It helps us to sort out our feelings and reactions to others and to come to feel closer to you, too.

Regular readers of our Kernel Books are increasingly beginning to feel at ease with us, to think of us as friends, to want to help us in our struggle to find understanding and the freedom to participate fully in all the things that make life joyous and complete.

Especially in these pages they have come to know and love and respect Dr. Kenneth Jernigan, who founded the Kernel Books, who edited the first fifteen of them, and whose warm, poignant, sparkling, and inspiring personal stories have formed the "Kernel" of every previous offering.

Which brings me to the present volume. We lost Kenneth Jernigan to cancer some months ago, and I am the new editor. From the time I was eighteen years old Dr. Jernigan was my teacher, my friend, my mentor—a dearly loved second father. I promised him I would do my best to carry on his work and particularly that I would see to it that the Kernel Books continued to help bring our sighted friends to share our hopes and dreams.

I have named this sixteenth volume in the series *Remember To Feed The Kittens* as a symbol and remembrance of the love and care Kenneth Jernigan unceasingly gave to all in need of his help. I watched him throughout his lifetime gather to him those who had no place in the world—be they human or stray kitten—and make them belong. He always remembered to feed the kittens. We and our ever-increasing number of sighted friends and colleagues will do the same.

Marc Maurer
Baltimore, Maryland
1999

The Colonies, the Court, and the Kittens

by Marc Maurer

There are oddities in the lives of blind people which are hard to explain, but we try to explain them anyway. One of these oddities happened to me in Williamsburg, Virginia.

When I was a boy, our family had very few vacations, as these are sometimes known today. Vacation had two meanings for us, in those days, and maybe it still does. Vacation meant the time school was not in session, but it also meant taking a trip for the purpose of enjoying the company of family members in unfamiliar places and circumstances.

Our family had plenty of the "not going to school" kind of vacations, but we were short on the other kind. We enjoyed being with each other just fine, but we almost never "went" on a vacation. Because this is the way I grew up, I have very few firmly established notions about what a vacation trip is supposed to offer. I am quite certain that vacation trips are supposed to be fun, but that is all.

Christmas is (for my family and me) the most important and joyous holiday of the year. I love the giving of presents and all of the planning that is a part of the preparation for the day. I also love the wonderful Christmas smells, the good food, and the togetherness. Christmas is important because it is a time for the expression of love for others and for the performance of small miracles. Bringing delight to the hearts of others is one of the fundamental purposes for this most joyous holiday.

Dr. Kenneth Jernigan served as president of the National Federation of the Blind for almost twenty years. He and his wife became a part of the Maurer family, sharing the Christmas holidays with all of the warmth and joy that they possess.

Dr. Jernigan loved Christmas and the Christmas season as much as the rest of us. However, he had died in October after a yearlong fight with cancer. I wondered how we could spend Christmas without him; I also wondered how Dr. Jernigan's wife Mary Ellen would face this first Christmas alone.

Although we would not want to change any of the Christmas traditions—a big Christmas dinner together, prayers, attendance at church, the exchanging of presents, and all that is a part of the holiday—I wondered if a change of setting for at least part of the Christmas season wouldn't be worthwhile.

Consequently, we decided—the Maurers and Mrs. Jernigan—to take a vacation between Christmas and New Years. We planned a visit to Williamsburg, Virginia, a place noted as the provincial capital of Virginia prior to the American Revolution.

Because the adult Maurers, my wife Patricia and I, are both blind, and because the children, David and Dianna, are not old enough for driver's licenses Mrs. Jernigan would drive. Two days after Christmas, we packed the essentials for the trip—handheld computer games designed for entertaining children riding in a car, a portable CD player with headphones for private music listening, several different kinds of Christmas candy, and (almost as an afterthought) a few clothes.

The Jernigan house is less than a block from our front door, and, as we carried our bags toward the departure point, we met two of Dr. Jernigan's kittens coming through the front gate into our yard. Some years ago Dr. Jernigan had adopted a family of stray kittens who had shown up in his yard. After that he always made a home for others who appeared from time to time.

I thought of him then, and seeing his kittens reminded me how he had always taught us to share whatever we had with others. I remembered what he had done for me and my family and for many other blind people who had had no place to be until he showed us how to hope and believe.

Blinking back the tears, I stopped for a moment to ask the kittens if they had had their breakfast, but they seemed in a hurry. When we reached the Jernigan house, we spoke to Mrs. Jernigan wondering if the kittens would be O.K. She told us she had made provision for them to be fed while we were away.

There had been an ice storm and a number of trees had fallen. These trees blocked the roadway and slowed our progress. Furthermore, the reports on the radio told us that Williamsburg and the surrounding area was without electricity. Fortunately, when we arrived our hotel had power. We would not have to use candles, and there would be hot water, operating elevators, and coffee.

Mrs. Jernigan and I stepped to the hotel check-in desk to fill out our room registration papers. Although I was standing before the desk, the clerk asked Mrs. Jernigan what kind of room I needed. Then she asked Mrs. Jernigan if I had any special requirements.

I myself responded to each question. However, the desk clerk seemed almost unaware of me. She asked Mrs. Jernigan if she would sign the registration for me. Then she questioned Mrs. Jernigan about how I would pay my bill. Again, I responded myself.

The peculiar nature of the conversation created some awkwardness. There are those who find blindness so threatening that they want to ignore it. Others believe that the blind are incapable of the most rudimentary activities, and they automatically assume that any sighted person in the company of a blind person is in charge.

We tried gently to persuade the desk clerk to understand that I myself am capable and responsible for my own family. I answered the questions put to Mrs. Jernigan as if they had been addressed to me. However, I was completely unprepared for the last of the questions. The desk clerk handed Mrs. Jernigan a parking pass to be placed on the dashboard of her car. Then, she asked Mrs. Jernigan if I had also driven to the hotel and if I would like a parking pass for my car.

I spent some time wondering how to account for this question. The desk clerk knew quite clearly that I was blind, yet she refused to speak to me. Nevertheless, she offered Mrs. Jernigan a parking pass for the car she thought I might have driven to the hotel. It reminded me that although we have made much progress, we still have a way to go in helping blind people achieve opportunity in America.

During our visit to Colonial Williamsburg, we participated in a reenactment of courtroom proceedings which had occurred more than 200 years earlier. As we stepped into the courtroom the bailiff said to us that jurors must be selected for the trial. The members of the jury were required to be adult, white, Protestant, able-bodied males. All others were prohibited from serving.

As I sat within the body of the court, I reflected that although I am a lawyer, I could not serve on the colonial jury of those days. The bailiff did not tell us whether my blindness would have prohibited me from representing clients in the court.

One of the cases that afternoon was brought against a man who had failed to go to church. The laws of Virginia in the 1770's required citizens of the state to attend the officially recognized Protestant church service at least one Sunday each month. The defendant in the case said he was a member of the Catholic faith and that his religion prohibited him from participation in Protestant worship.

During the course of the trial it was argued that his attendance at the Protestant service would be a mortal sin which would subject him to eternal damnation. As I listened to the presentation of each of the parties involved, I thought about how I would defend this Catholic if I had been his lawyer, and I wondered whether I would have been permitted to plead the case.

The King's representative in court pointed out to the jurors that church service was not merely a religious matter but a secular one as well. Edicts from the Crown, from the House of Burgesses, or the local city fathers would be read at church. Consequently, it was the civic duty of every citizen to be in attendance.

Although the position of the parties seemed irreconcilable, I could imagine myself attempting to touch the hearts of the jurors. The very arguments of the King's counsel, it seemed to me, suggested that if the civic duty could be met, there would be no need for the Catholic to participate in the Protestant worship service.

The argument that the civic duty was important implied that the law had been established to serve the government rather than God. If God were being served in some other way, this should satisfy the court.

As we left Williamsburg on our way back to Baltimore, I thought about how far we as blind people have come and how far we must still travel to become self-sufficient. I am a practicing lawyer today, and I have been summoned for jury service. In Colonial Williamsburg I might have been a minstrel, a storyteller, or a beggar; but I would probably not have had the opportunity for other employment.

Nevertheless despite my learning and ability, sometimes I find that the desk clerk will refuse to speak to me because I am blind. We must help people come to be at ease with those of us who are blind. In the National Federation of the Blind we are making an effort to bring this change into being. We appreciate our friends, and we hope to find more of them. We are willing to work and to learn, and sometimes we will take a vacation. We will do it for ourselves and our friends, but as we do it, we will remember to feed the kittens, too.

Michael Baillif

A ROOF WITH A VIEW

by Michael Baillif

Michael Baillif is a past president of the Student Division of the National Federation of the Blind. In his college years he received help through our scholarship program. Today he is a successful lawyer, specializing in corporate taxes. He is employed by a major New York City law firm—which, by the way, sought out Michael's services because of his growing professional reputation in his specialty.

In his story, A Roof With A View, *Michael, who is still a young man, looks back to a time when he was an even younger man. Fifteen to be exact. Fifteen and in love. At one level it is a delightful, lighthearted story. At another it expresses the poignant yearning of a young man who is blind for physical independence and spiritual self-sufficiency. Here is what he has to say:*

I was fifteen years old when I fell in love for the first time. The condition of being fifteen years old and in love presents a variety of imperatives that cannot be ignored. Deep heartfelt sighs, long solitary walks, and interminable conversations with friends all about "her" are among the rituals that must be observed.

I had become blind the year before and had not yet received meaningful training in the alternative skills needed to succeed as a blind person. Indeed I had never even met another blind person to whom I could look as a role model. Nevertheless, I was functioning reasonably well as a teenager in love.

One balmy summer evening I took it into my head that I should write some poetry and that the only place suitable for such a solemn and spiritual undertaking was on the roof of my house. This determination presented a challenge that was both frightening and exhilarating. The problem was straight-forward: how to get onto the roof in the first instance and then, once there, how to get down again without suffering bodily harm.

Other issues presented themselves as well. I could not ask for help or advice in reaching my goal. In addition, my ascent to the roof had to be done in secret, thus avoiding the need for bothersome explanations. That's how it is when you're fifteen years old and in love.

As a result the simple expedient of dragging a ladder up to one end of the house and leaning it against the roof was out of the question. Instead, more creativity was required. After much thought and exploration, I hit on the solution.

A trellis reaching to within a few feet of the roof ran along one corner of the house. I formulated a scheme whereby I would sneak a chair out of the kitchen and position it behind the trellis. I could stand on the chair and then jump up to catch the top of the trellis, on which there was a six-inch platform.

From that precarious perch, I could turn and pull myself up onto the roof.

I was satisfied that this approach allowed reasonable odds of achieving the rooftop. Nevertheless, still more logistical issues needed to be considered. First, the roof was a shingled A-frame roof that rose sharply from the eaves to the apex. The footing was uncertain, and there were a number of obstacles such as vents, antennae wires, and a chimney, all presenting hazards to the unwary.

Moreover, there was the question of how to get back down in some way other than a headlong crash. The trellis was only a few feet long; and, if I veered only slightly in either the ascent or descent from the pinnacle of the roof, I could miss it altogether and end up stranded.

I decided that these problems could best be solved through the use of a telescoping cane. It could be carried in my backpack as I climbed up the trellis and then taken out for use once I reached the roof. The cane would help me locate obstacles on the roof; and, when it came time for my return to terra firma, I could swing the cane over the edge of the roof until it located the trellis.

I generally incorporated the cane into my day-to-day life as little as possible because it was a symbol of blindness with which I was not yet comfortable. Nevertheless, in this case I had a goal, and the cane was the tool that would allow me to achieve it.

After formulating my plans and drawing inspiration from one last thought of my beloved, I put the scheme into action. I sneaked the chair out of the kitchen without detection, and, but for a few perilous moments when I nearly tumbled helter-skelter over the opposite end of the trellis, I attained the roof.

Then, according to plan, I pulled out my cane and climbed cautiously to the roof's apex. There, taking care not to roll backwards down the other side of the roof, I found a comfortable and reasonably secure place from which to enjoy the evening and compose my poetry.

From the height of the rooftop and from my perspective as a fifteen-year-old, I surveyed the world and liked what I saw. I was in love; and, feeling the urge to climb the roof and write poetry, I had done so despite the fear and uncertainty that had been ever-present throughout the adventure.

Later I would need the guidance and support of my friends in the National Federation of the Blind to develop and mold this inherent desire for physical independence and spiritual self-sufficiency that yearned to come forth. But climbing the roof represented the first tentative steps along the path that would bring me into contact with these friends whom I did not even know existed but whom I so desperately needed.

I wrote poetry late into that summer evening and would have labored longer except that the batteries in the tape recorder into which I was dictating my verses began to run low. Had I known then how to use a slate and stylus to write Braille, I might have stayed on the rooftop until sunrise.

After dictating some final lines into the dying tape recorder, I pulled out my cane and started the painstaking descent down the roof toward the trellis. Upon reaching the edge of the roof, I swung my cane over the side and held my breath; it touched nothing but air. I moved a few feet in one direction along the edge of the roof—still nothing! I then went back in the other direction and, to my vast relief, located the trellis with my cane. From there I completed my return to earth without incident.

At the time I was convinced that I carried off my entire adventure without my parents' notice. Although this may have been the case, as I now better understand the extent of my parents' wisdom, I suspect that they knew all along but simply kept their own counsel.

The last I heard, the object of my romantic attentions was somewhere in Australia, married to a fellow named "Mr. Wright." To this day, however, I can feel the touch of the warm evening breeze and hear the far-off sound of crickets and feel again the surge of triumph and satisfaction that I experienced that long ago summer night when I sat atop a roof composing poetry just like any other fifteen-year-old in love.

IT'S A CAT'S LIFE

by Peggy Elliott

Doug and Peggy Elliott are both blind and live in Grinnell, Iowa. When they invited a tiny blind kitten to join them and their two sighted, older cats awhile ago, they told Kernel Book readers about little Sheriff and her insistence on being left alone to explore and do for herself. Now Peggy, who also serves as Second Vice President of the National Federation of the Blind, brings us up-to-date on the growing blind cat, Sheriff.

Although it's hard to say for sure what Sheriff's adventures tell us about blindness, there is no question what they tell us about the Elliott household: It's a great place to be a cat! And perhaps it only stands to reason that a blind cat would try to make the same adaptations to cat life as a blind human does to human living. In any case, for cat lovers, it is a delightful story. Here is what Peggy has to say:

Our little blind kitten has grown into a 9-pound teen-ager, tomboy, and endless source of amusement and pleasure. When we last reported about Sheriff, she was a newcomer to our house, recently retrieved from the vet who had cured all her outside-kitty parasites and given us soothing ointment for her infected eyes. Soothing is all we could do; Sheriff cannot see.

This has never bothered Sheriff. She's constantly busy. Most cats play with an object for a while and then lose it. Sheriff picks favorite toys and keeps them around for weeks. The most recent one is a mouse with a bell on its tail. She'll smack it, chase it down, capture it, and smack again. When the game is over for a time, she'll leave it.

The thing about her, though, is that she remembers where. Later, you'll see her carrying it in her mouth to a new hockey area or hear the bell jingling in another room. Now we think one of the older cats has finally stolen and hidden the mouse. But Sheriff always finds another toy.

Doug Elliott and Sheriff

Cellophane packages are another favorite, and Wednesday grocery day with all the fresh sacks on the floor is a highlight of the week for Sheriff. She hasn't done this for awhile, but she used to find a sack, put her front paws and shoulders in, lie down, and push herself and the sack forward while making a prrt prrt prrt sound for all the world like a little feline motorboat. When the sack would hit the cabinets and stop, she would go to find another and repeat the process.

Toys are an important part of Sheriff's day. Of course anything she plays with has to make or create sound. I think it's fair to say her very favorite toys are Doug and me.

When she was tiny, Sheriff spent hours climbing up and down the ladders on our ladderbacked kitchen chairs. When she would reach the top, she would balance there, all four feet on the top rung, very pleased with herself and sometimes bold enough to bat at a passing human toy.

She's too big now to do this climbing act; she'd just knock the chair over if she tried. So she's modified the game. Now she puts her back feet on the seat of an empty chair and her front paws on the top rung. She positions herself there when a human toy is going to pass and then bats out at you, swatting accurately at Doug or me as we pass.

It's amazing what Sheriff can find that fits the sound-making toy bill. One of us got a small electrical appliance, a tape recorder or something, that came packed in styrofoam peanuts. We already knew about Sheriff's love of peanuts. They make nice scratching sounds as they move across a surface.

This particular box with the peanuts got set under the bed in our bedroom and forgotten. Little Sheriff is always looking at her world and the details of her world with her paws. She goes places and finds stuff the two older cats never do. One day she found the box.

The first we knew about Sheriff's discovery was when she arrived on the bed with a peanut and began hitting it around, chasing it, pouncing, hitting, all while two humans were trying to get a little sleep.

One of us took the peanut away and put it under a pillow as a temporary fix. Sheriff followed the sound of the peanut and looked with her paws on and then around and then under the pillow. The peanut was too far under for her to find.

Little dejected (we thought) Sheriff hopped off the bed and, after a little time had passed, began batting another styrofoam peanut around the floor. I can't even begin to tell you how annoying the sound of a styrofoam peanut and a joyful cat can be in the middle of the night. This went on for days.

I don't know how many times she kept us awake playing on the floor and how many times we got bounced by her frisking on the bed and how many styrofoam peanuts we confiscated before we found the forgotten box.

And the little creep was clever enough to get the next one only after a pause so that we weren't sure what the distance was from her supply to the torture chamber that the bedroom had become while she had access to the endless supply. It's gone now, and we're careful to throw all peanuts away the minute they come in the house. She loves them as toys, but we like our sleep more.

It is constantly interesting to watch Sheriff exploring her environment. We got a new couch and love seat a few weeks ago, and Sheriff was immediately there, feeling, jumping, using her paws to see the outlines.

She's the first cat of our three that found that the backs are wide and padded enough to accommodate a sprawled, sleeping cat comfortably. She's appropriated the love seat as hers, and I've never seen either older cat up there.

When she was still a kitten, Sheriff showed us that she has a clear map of the world around her in her mind. We had a recliner set at right angles to a couch with a coffee table in front of the couch. Sheriff would get on Doug's knee in the recliner, reach out with her paw to find the edge of the coffee table, hop to the table, and then hop to the couch.

After a while, we decided the coffee table was too much in that setting and removed it. For weeks thereafter, Sheriff would get on Doug's knee, reach for the edge of the coffee table, reach farther, lean way out, wave around with her paw. She was convinced for a long time that she just wasn't reaching far enough since she knew there was a surface there.

She's stopped doing it now, but she did it so many times we had to conclude that she really remembered the table.

Sheriff is not afraid to try new routes. In an area she is not sure about, she checks with a paw before stepping. But then she remembers the pattern for later. Our front stairs turn twice, and our back stairs turn once. At the top and bottom of both, one must pick angles to arrive at different locations.

Sheriff has taken to racing people up and down the stairs and winning. In the morning, she waits at the top of the front stairs, usually used by the first person up. When one of us starts down, she leaps into motion, races ahead, and invariably beats us to the kitchen. She's running all the way.

We tied a string on a knob of my dresser as a cat toy. Neither older cat has to my knowledge so much as looked at the string. For about nine months, the string formed part of Sheriff's morning ritual. She would flop down on the floor under the string and commence to swat, bite, kick, and roll in reaction to and activation of the string.

The game would last for ten to fifteen minutes a day, and she kept this up for about nine months. She's tired of that game now and doesn't do it anymore. But it's clear that she intentionally went to the string each morning, knowing where it was and how to play the game.

Once Sheriff got caught in a little dead-end hallway off the main upstairs hall. GirlKitty (one of the older cats) was standing at the mouth of the dead-end, growling at her. I stepped over GirlKitty and started downstairs.

Then it occurred to me that there was a reason why GirlKitty, the only Sheriff hater I know, was growling. She was penning Sheriff in the dead-end. I stopped about three steps down and reached through the widely-spaced rails into the dead-end. Sheriff was sitting right on the edge. I petted her and went on down a few more stairs. Then I heard Sheriff flop onto the stairs. She had figured out that, if I was there, she could be there, too.

She didn't quite know the distances, but she did know that she had been trapped and that I had showed her, she thought, a way out. She hasn't taken that route since, but she was braver at trying than I probably would have been with the same information she had.

Speaking of how Sheriff thinks reminds me of the shrimp. We were having boiled shrimp one night, and we decided to put an empty bowl over the tails in the tail bowl as a protection against marauding cats. All three know they are not supposed to be on the table and steal food, but, well, you know cats.

If you leave an unusually juicy morsel unguarded, you have to take your chances. So we devised the tail bowl protector to save ourselves the trouble. First we heard the bowl being investigated and moved a bit, followed by a disappointed Bobby (the other older cat) leaving the table with his trademark "prrrt" as he jumps.

Then the sounds were repeated followed by the more clumsy and non-verbal exit of GirlKitty. Then no sound for awhile.

Doug reached over to put a tail in the bowl and discovered little Sheriff industriously working on uncracking the puzzle. She had examined the container with the good smells very carefully with her front paws and had gotten one paw in between the lips of the two bowls. When Doug happened to reach over, Sheriff had the two bowls separated and was working her nose into the widening gap.

She had unlocked the puzzle neither older, sighted cat had had the patience or persistence to deconstruct and was about to graze upon the ambrosia easily withheld from both older cats. Though I don't specifically remember, I can guess that either Doug or I rewarded her persistence after we removed her from the table.

And then there are the dropped things in the kitchen. When a human is in the kitchen, Sheriff is usually there too, just in case. She wouldn't want to withhold an opportunity from a human to give her treats. To be fair, she usually hangs around one of us wherever we are. But, back to the kitchen.

Anything you drop, from an ice cube to a spoon to a few kernels of frozen corn escaped from the bag. Anything. If Sheriff is in the kitchen, she will probably find it more quickly than we do. The minute something hits the floor, she leaps into action, using her ears and her knowledge of the kitchen to run right to the dropped thing and "kill" it.

She seems to understand that these things are not usually subject to the game of cat hockey. It's just a mere matter of finding. And she likes to race to the dropped object, being the first to find it. She's even come tearing in from the dining room, around the refrigerator and into the end of the kitchen to find something.

Now that we know the game, it's a matter of pride to find the dropped thing before the cat does. But I would say that the score is about 50-50 even though the human doing the dropping is usually closer when the drop occurs. Sheriff's good.

The most fun thing of all about Sheriff, though, is her intense conviction that she can communicate. Some of the communication, of course, deals with food. We recycle cans after washing them in the dishwasher and store them in the back hallway for the weekly city pick-up.

When Sheriff was quite little, she dug an empty, dishwashed tuna can out of the recycling bin and carried it over to Doug's feet, dropping it there as a statement of desire.

Sheriff has never repeated that ploy since it didn't work. But when someone opens the refrigerator, you may find Sheriff there, standing on her back legs and touching the tuna can sitting on the second shelf at the left. She is always ready to let us know just where it is.

Sheriff also knows that her bell gives her away. Most of the time, you can hear the bell merrily ringing as Sheriff trots along or rolls over during a nap. Sometimes you'd swear she's intentionally ringing the bell louder when she's happy and running around.

But there are other times when the bell goes silent. Then you find a little cat nose or paw where it's not supposed to be.

As I say, Sheriff is certain she can communicate her wishes. She likes to snuggle down in bed against one of us for the night. She has a favorite place next to Doug, and she's sometimes ready for sleep before we are. Every now and then we'll be talking, and a sleepy paw will appear very gently on Doug's mouth. The message is clear.

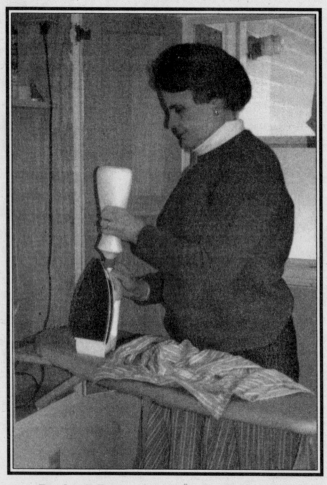

Barbara Pierce doing the family ironing

THIS IS THE WAY WE WASH OUR CLOTHES

by Barbara Pierce

As regular Kernel Book readers know, Barbara Pierce is president of the National Federation of the Blind of Ohio, the mother of three grown children, the wife of a college English professor, an accomplished homemaker, and the writer of delightful stories that sparkle with wit and wisdom. Her current offering is no exception. Here is what she has to say:

Do you recall the children's song called, I seem to remember, "This is the Way We Wash Our Clothes"? In successive verses singers work their way through the days of the week demonstrating with motions the way we wash our clothes, iron our clothes, mend our clothes, sweep the floor, and bake the bread.

With the ironing board and the broom nearly extinct today and the bread machine creating most of the fresh bread in modern homes, perhaps children no longer take delight in singing this little tune. On the other hand, I had very little idea of what a wash board was when I was a child, yet we vigorously mimed washing our clothes on a wash board. It never occurred to us to wonder where the washing machine had disappeared to in the song.

I had a bit of vision when I was a small child, but not enough to pick up the motions that went with the song by observing the leader or the other children.

My mother carefully taught me how to move my hands and arms and also what those motions represented. I suspect I may have been the only child in my group who knew that those pushing gestures in the Thursday verse represented kneading the bread.

But Mother wasn't satisfied simply to teach me to go through the motions of taking care of a home; she insisted that I learn how to be an effective member of the family. Once I overcame my initial annoyance at being forced to do chores around the house, I have always been grateful that she invested the effort to teach me to be self-sufficient.

How does one do the laundry without looking at the job? The secret of efficient clothes washing is proper sorting. But how does a blind person accurately sort colors and fabrics? The answer is by touch.

My first laundry task as a small child was to collect my father's dress shirts for their trip to the laundry, where the collars could be starched stiff, the way Dad liked them. I liked the stiff collars too, because it was easy to find them quickly in the dirty clothes hamper.

The rest of the laundry got sorted on the basement floor. Underwear and sheets could go together. Jeans, wash pants, and boys' and men's socks formed the basis of another pile. Obviously delicate fabrics made a third stack.

With those things out of the way, I was left with all the pieces that might be light colored or might be dark. There was nothing to do but learn to identify them. I quickly discovered that I already knew the colors of my own clothes. I knew what I had worn in recent days and thrown into the wash.

For the rest of the family I had to memorize the colors by identifying texture, buttons, and location of pockets and zippers. In the early days Mother checked to see that I had sorted the loads correctly, but eventually we learned to trust my own decisions. After all, if I really wasn't sure in which pile a garment belonged, I could leave it out for later consultation.

Naturally I had to learn the hard way to check for crayons in pockets. But all of us have discovered to our sorrow what happens when a red crayon melts in the dryer all over a load of light-colored clothes.

Actually, throughout all the years of laundry for my own three children, I had surprisingly few of these catastrophes. This is undoubtedly because my fingers pay close attention to information like a bit of extra weight or a hard object in a pocket under several layers of cloth.

Like every other washing machine in the nation, mine has always tended to eat socks. I cannot imagine where so many single socks can disappear in a load of wash. Before I discovered the solution to this problem, we had a designated orphan drawer in our house. All unmated socks that came through the wash went into that drawer. In an emergency a desperate child could usually assemble a passable pair of socks from the extras.

Then I decided to take radical action. I couldn't match a dryer full of single socks anyway, so I put a bowl of safety pins in the bathroom and told everybody to pin socks together before they went into the laundry baskets.

I promised that, if socks were pinned, they would be returned to the owner folded together. If they went through the wash one by one, they would be dumped into the orphan drawer. Everyone soon learned that it was simpler to pin the socks together than to brave the sock drawer in search of something to wear.

I said earlier that the ironing board is almost extinct in America. I certainly don't iron nearly as much as my mother did or as I did when I was a kid. But mine still gets a fair workout, even today. Partly this is because I have the luxury of a laundry room on the second floor. It is a converted sun porch.

When we first moved to our home, built in 1891, I found myself carrying laundry from the bathroom at the back of the second floor to the staircase at the front of the house and then back to the basement steps at the rear of the first floor. Our house is large—thirteen rooms—and our then toddler was frightened to be left alone while I went off to feed the washer and dryer. So I usually carried not only the dirty clothes but also the squirmy baby whenever I made this extended trip.

It was great exercise, but I began to have fantasies about having the washer and dryer on the second floor. That is where they have been now for twenty years, and it is a lovely arrangement. The only drawback is that I am tempted to toss a load into the washer late in the evening and into the dryer just before tumbling into bed. The result is wrinkles.

Actually I rather enjoy ironing. I don't burn myself more than occasionally. The iron radiates enough heat to tell my left hand exactly where it is. With just a bit of practice, it is easy to determine by touch whether the wrinkles have disappeared. And, if I accidentally press in a crease, a spritz of water allows me to press it out again.

I fill my steam iron with distilled water to prevent stains from mineral deposits on the clothes. Using a funnel, I put the water into a clean dish-washing-liquid bottle. The nozzle lid on my recycled plastic bottle allows me to invert it over the iron's water well before opening the nozzle and squeezing out enough water to fill the iron.

I can hear the well filling, but even if it overflows a bit, holding the iron flat for a moment allows it to spit out the excess before I put it down on the fabric.

This is the way blind people wash our clothes and iron our clothes and take care of our families. Is it any different from the way other people do the job? Not really.

The members of the National Federation of the Blind aren't amazing. There is nothing magic about learning to adjust to blindness. It takes a bit of time and some practice to train your fingers and ears to do the things that other people do with sight, but it can be done. We know because we've done it.

Tonia Trapp

OF MICE AND REFRIGERATORS

by Tonia Trapp

Regular readers of the Kernel Book series will find the following story to be a marked change of pace. It contains no special insights about blindness, exposes no wrongs to be righted, seeks to teach no lessons. Why then, do I include it? I do so merely because I thought you might enjoy this young woman's fanciful account of cleaning out the refrigerator as much as I did. Here it is:

Two days ago, at about 12:30 p.m., I bounded up the basement stairs from my bedroom and into the kitchen. It was lunchtime—time to scrounge something up from amongst the dizzying array of containers cooling in our refrigerator. Mom was not home, so I was on my own. Sighing, I attempted mentally to prepare myself for the task ahead of me.

Flinging open the refrigerator door, I began to examine the contents of the shelves, opening one container after another. Since I cannot see, I conducted my examination in two ways: first, I would sniff. If that did not clearly indicate to me what was inside, then it was time to reach into the container, poking and prodding—at clear risk to myself—to find out what was there.

For a while, things were going well. I discovered that we had one piece of lasagna left, just enough for me. How grand! This was just what I had been looking for. I also found some pickles and a leftover fish mixture that might be a fine complement to my lasagna.

Satisfied and happy, I surveyed the containers sitting on the counter that held my soon-to-be-eaten lunch. And then, it occurred to me. Mom had not cleaned out the refrigerator in weeks. It was time for me to help her out. I am the only one who is usually brave enough to do this. Perhaps that is because I can not see what lurks stealthily behind closed lids and therefore have no conception of the risks that I take when I decide to fulfill my self-inflicted duties of Kitchen Executor.

Now, why I didn't just stop there, zap my lunch in the microwave and leave the refrigerator clean-up chore for some one else, I have no idea. But something within me compelled me to continue to probe the depths of what I instinctively knew would disgust me. So I plunged in.

I started with the bottom shelf. Ah ha! That plastic bag with two rolls in it was still tucked cozily into the back corner. Last time I had pulled these out, three weeks ago, my mother had insisted that we were definitely going to eat those. Didn't happen. "These <u>must</u> be moldy by now," I thought. So out they came.

Then I moved to the next shelf above that. I found the same cylindrical, screw-top contraption that had been there a month and a half ago. Then, its contents had smelled like liver—something I absolutely despise. Now, I pulled out the container and sniffed it again. Hmm . . . doesn't smell like anything. Oh no! No smell, no clue—that means I'll have actually to <u>touch</u> what's in there.

"OK, Tonia," I pep-talked myself, "you must be brave, now. Think of the good you are doing, the lives you are saving." I reached in and found a hardened mass of what felt like hamburger meat but which, surely, was not. "Interesting," I mused, "that fascinating mass of inedible glop seems to have shrunk over the past six weeks." And so it had.

I continued my painstaking work, which soon led me to extract a dozen or so tiny plastic vessels that could each hold only enough to feed a mouse family of four. When I stuck my hand into one of these, I found, to my utmost horror, a solidified, slime-ified substance at the bottom that repulsed me so much that I threw down the vessel and cried out in agony, "No, no, no! Yuck! That's so nasty. Why is this happening to me? What did I do to deserve this?" I marched to the garbage pail with container in hand and shook out the slime creature inside. But wait, part of it hadn't quite made it into the bag but was hanging over the edge! I had to slide it all the way into the bag, and as I did so, I lamented loudly that now part of the bag was covered with the slime that I wished so much to escape. "Please," I whispered to the uncomprehending slop in the pail, "don't hurt me."

As I opened more of these mouse-feast-sized containers, I came to the conclusion that over time, their contents do indeed solidify and, in some cases, slime-ify. I realized something else, too. The smaller containers are the ones that tend to get emptied last in my house, so they stay in our refrigerator longer than anything else.

It must be, I thought to myself, that my mother, poor dear soul, is under the delusion that the smaller the container, the longer its contents will last. Because of this, we own a bewildering profusion of tiny vessels of all shapes and sizes—and these, needless to say, are constantly crowding and filling our refrigerator.

I wonder, now that I think about it, if there isn't some kind of conspiracy going on. Perhaps several thousand mouse families living in our house periodically tuck snacks away for themselves in our conveniently sized mouse-feast containers. This would explain why these receptacles fill our fridge, and it would also explain why their contents shrink and slime-ify so quickly. Everyone knows that mice are slimy little slicks, isn't that right?

So what if my theory is true. What then? Well, I was just going to go shopping soon, so while I'm at the grocery store, I'll just pick up some more cold cuts. Oh, and we're running out of small containers. They're all filled up at the moment. Better get some more.

Cars, Teen-agers, And Insurance

by Ramona Walhof

Dealing with teen-age drivers presents challenges or any parent: What car will the teen-ager drive and ow to acquire it? What about insurance? What bout learning how to drive? Are these challenges the ame or different if the parent happens to be blind? hese are the questions Ramona Walhof, who is resident of the National Federation of the Blind f Idaho, deals with in her story, Cars, Teen-agers, nd Insurance.

As readers of earlier Kernel Books will remember, Ramona became a widow when her two children were ery young. Now they are both young adults, finished ith college, and launched in their careers. As a matter f fact, each of them has wedding plans for this year. Here is what Ramona has to say:

n 1983 I was 39 years old, working as Director of a State Rehabilitation Program

for the Blind, a single mother of two childre
ages 12 and 13, and it came time for me t
buy my first car.

I had saved money and thought I neede
a van. I wanted to take my children place
and include their friends. I wanted to tak
groups of students on trips. I wanted to tak
groups of blind people to activities of th
National Federation of the Blind. I ha
sighted drivers available, so the time had com

I asked my assistant if he could spare
Saturday to drive me around and give m
some advice. He said he would be glad t
drive but wasn't sure how much advice h
could give. This was reasonable. I knew
would have to look before buying. We spen
the whole day looking at a lot of vehicle
most of which I did not want. Many were se
up as campers or did not have enough seats.
wanted 15 seats. I saw three vans I liked, an
two were very plush. I was looking fo
something utilitarian.

*The Walhofs—Ramona, Laura,
and Christopher*

Near the end of the day, we found a Plymouth Voyager that seemed right. We were pretty sure it was the only one in Boise, but I didn't want to offer too high. I had to learn about the negotiations. The salesman didn't really believe I was buying the van. He tried to talk to my assistant who simply waved at me and said he wasn't buying it.

I made my offer, which was cash, and I could tell they were interested, but not ready to accept. The salesman disappeared to talk with his supervisor, but said almost nothing. I believe I was the only serious customer in the store that afternoon about 5:00 p.m. I could not tell whether they were reluctant to deal with me because I was blind and female or for some other reason, but they were uncomfortable.

Soon the supervisor came back and tried to talk to my assistant who wasn't responsive. Then the supervisor told me that their price was a very good one. I said that maybe it was, but I would not go any higher. The supervisor wanted to know who would be driving the van, and shouldn't he or she have something to say about it? I answered that a number of people would be driving the van, but I was buying it, and he had to deal with me. Both men disappeared, and I called a friend, thinking we were going to come to terms and would need another driver.

I wasn't sure whether the salesman and supervisor were more worried about the price or the blindness. Then they came back and agreed to accept my price. As we proceeded through the paperwork, I was becoming excited.

When Harry and Jan arrived, the supervisor immediately began to talk to Harry as though the van were his. Harry directed the comments back to me. Harry was asked: "Aren't you her husband?"

Jan answered: "No, he's _my_ husband."

They just couldn't believe a blind woman could or should buy a van. I was grateful to my friends who were members of the National Federation of the Blind and helped me deal with the attitudes of the salesman and the supervisor.

Jan and Harry Gawith and my assistant, John Cheadle, knew exactly how to respond when they were addressed, even though I was the customer. This made my van-buying experience easier and more enjoyable. We got the job done, and I then had to learn about insurance.

Later, I found that new cars are generally insured by the seller for 48 to 72 hours, but I didn't know that then. So Saturday night I thought I had to find insurance. Of course, we did not want to wait until Monday to drive this wonderful new van! Harry would be driving the van some and had a good driving record. So I called his agent who agreed that Harry could be the primary driver.

We used the van as planned for more than year. Then I changed employment and arted a bakery, and we also used the van for liveries.

At that time in Idaho, teen-agers could be ensed to drive during daylight hours at age ourteen. My daughter Laura was most nxious to take driver's education. I knew that arting to drive a 15-passenger van was not a ery good idea. Still, that was the vehicle we ad needed when we bought it.

I found a driver's ed teacher who agreed o give her an extra lesson or two in the van, nd my assistant also was willing to work with er. Soon Laura took driver's ed, and the acher thought she was ready. She got her ense.

I decided there would be some special les. The State said Laura could not drive ter dark until she was sixteen. I decided she ust only drive with me or an adult driver in e van. When Spring came and the days were longer, I began letting her take the van by herself on certain errands. Still, she was n to use the van as transportation for her frienc unless I was in it.

One Saturday afternoon she went to ru some errands and then to band practice. Sl was more than an hour late getting home. H explanation was that a lot of her frienc needed rides home, and she had this bi vehicle. She could not refuse to help out. Sl had disregarded a very specific rule.

I told her to consider alternatives, but sl could not think of any. She had not though of a telephone. She had not thought c stopping at home to pick me up or talk abou what to do. She got one warning. I thought van full of teen-agers behind a driver so youn was dangerous. Teen-agers spend too muc energy entertaining one another, which distracting to any driver.

Although Laura had had her license abou six months, I wasn't sure she was ready fc that. Laura must have believed me when I told her that a repeat offense would make her a retired driver because it did not happen again.

Another time Laura came home late and did not have to be questioned about the problem. She had taken the wrong approach to the interstate and could not get off. When she found an exit in the next town, she had no idea how to get back on the freeway.

This is not a new experience for most drivers, but Laura clearly needed to learn the local interstate system, and I was not the best person to teach her. We chose a time when we were not in a hurry and took my son Chris along. Although Chris was still too young to drive, he was a good sign reader. We practiced on freeway entrances and exits, and Laura got over being frightened.

Another tense moment occurred one Sunday afternoon when we were shopping at Sears. Laura said: "Let's park in the garage."

Before I could suggest caution, she had turned in. There was no trouble parking the van, but when we were ready to leave, there was. Laura rubbed the side of the van against a pole and scratched it. She didn't know how to get away from the pole in the restricted space. As people began to line up behind us, she became upset.

A stranger got out of one of the cars behind us and offered to help. Fortunately, he knew exactly what to do and inched the van away from the post. With relief and an ugly scratch on our van, we left the garage, and Laura no longer had a fascination with parking garages.

During that first summer after Laura got her driver's license, I took her with me on business trips to Idaho Falls (300 miles from Boise) and to Spokane (400 miles away). Perhaps I should say I used her as a driver on these trips, and we both enjoyed it. It was good experience for Laura and helpful to me.

I could tell that she was gaining in skill and confidence.

About that time they tore up the road in front of our bakery, and I decided to close it. Then we began to get numerous requests to borrow the van. Apparently people got the idea that we weren't using it much. We really didn't need so large a vehicle any more, so I decided it was time to trade for a smaller car.

I took Laura and Chris to look for a small car, and we agreed on a GLC Mazda. The salesman had no trouble dealing with me, but many people behaved as though the car belonged to Laura. I thought she was too young to have a car, and I intended to manage its use. Laura may have faced some pressure from her friends and others, but she lived within the system.

Now the question of insurance was more complex. Laura was not the primary driver, but she was the only driver in the household. Again, I turned to a friend in the National

Federation of the Blind. Mary Ellen Halverson and her husband were both blind and had a sighted son who was the only driver in their household.

Mary Ellen told me how they handled car insurance and gave me the name of their agent. I contacted that agent who agreed, after consultation, that it was possible to name Laura as the secondary driver and my business associate as the primary driver. So that is what we did.

Then Chris took driver's education and got his license. I made the same kinds of rules for Chris as I had for Laura. I was able to use him as a driver during the summer when I made trips out of town. He did not have to learn to drive the van, and he turned out to be quite a good driver. But the insurance agent was having a hard time saying that there were two drivers in the household, and neither was the primary driver.

It was true, but it was so unusual that it was not believed. I wrote up a schedule of how I used the car in my business while Chris and Laura were in school. The insurance company listed the drivers as they should: business associate, primary driver; Laura, secondary driver; and Chris, secondary driver.

When Chris was in ninth grade, he had a paper route. Although he could do it on foot or on his bike, he preferred to drive, especially on Sundays when the papers were large. When he drove, I would go along and put rubber bands on the papers.

One morning a police car pulled us over. What, we wondered, could it mean? "Why don't you have your lights on?" the policeman asked. He didn't wait for an answer. He must have seen the newspapers in the back seat because he said, "Did you just pull out of a brightly lit intersection?" We had.

"Don't forget to turn on your lights," he said and waved us on. He didn't even ask to see Chris' license. If he had, he probably would have had to write a ticket. It was still dark, and Chris was too young to drive in the dark. I'm sure it helped that I was in the car, and I'm sure Chris did not forget lights when he needed them after that.

By the end of her junior year in high school, Laura had been driving 3 years, and Chris one. Laura had been riding to school with a friend and her mother since the city bus did not start early enough in the morning, and the school bus did not stop at our corner.

We lived about one and a half miles from school, but there were always band instruments, piles of books, and other things to carry back and forth. Furthermore, schedules for two high school students were complicated. I never intended to let my high school kids drive to school, but it seemed the best way to go.

We started reading ads in the newspaper to find a small used pick-up. After looking at and driving several, we found a 1976 Datsun with a reconditioned second engine for $800. I decided to take a chance on it. It turned out to be the right decision. Laura and Chris drove that truck for 3 years. We replaced the battery, the tires, and the ignition and nothing else. Its performance was amazingly good. Now I had two vehicles.

I wanted to insure the truck (liability only) with Laura and Chris as the drivers. The Mazda was still mine, and I used it far more than either Chris or Laura. The policy came back with Chris on one vehicle and Laura on the other. That's the standard way, and the insurance company didn't believe you could have two drivers and two cars in one household and not insure them with one name on each vehicle. With the help of our agent, the insurance company finally was convinced.

After high school graduation, Laura went to college at Massachusetts Institute of

Technology in Boston and did not need a car. We all agreed on that.

Two years later when Chris enrolled at the University of Idaho in Moscow, we decided a car was reasonable. Chris enjoyed driving, and other transportation was limited. The little Datsun pick-up, I was afraid, might not be reliable enough for the 300-mile trip several times a year.

Chris and I bought a used Renault Fuego. That was a mistake. He loved it. It went fast! He must have controlled the speed, because I never heard about any tickets. But he only drove it one year. We couldn't get parts to repair the transmission, and that was the end of it.

Chris had decided to do door-to-door sales during the summers to help pay his way through school, so I wanted him to have a car that could be worked on absolutely anywhere. The Fuego helped me learn this lesson. In high school, Chris had shown no interest in what was under the hood of a car, but in college he did. We replaced the Fuego with a Ford Escort wagon.

At first he wasn't sure he was a "wagon man." He drove that Ford Escort for almost four years and put another 100,000 miles on it. He got good use out of the car. Those summers away from home selling books helped Chris grow up, and learning about engines, mechanics, tires, etc. was a part of it.

Meanwhile I had traded the Mazda for a 1987 Dodge 600 which is a little larger. It carries six people instead of four. This is still my car today. By the time I bought it, I felt I had learned how to shop for a car.

But Chris and Laura still had a few more challenges for me. When Laura graduated from college, she needed a vehicle. I decided that would be her graduation present and my last financial contribution to her education. She wanted a red pick-up, but did not want to pay the extra insurance premium. She had a teaching job at a school in the Chicago area, so we needed to move boxes and some furniture from Boise and from Boston to Chicago. We found a used Ford Ranger (blue) that seemed O.K. She drove it hard for two years and was able to trade it for a new Saturn.

The four years of driving during high school were important to Laura. She was not a natural driver and needed the practice. If she had gone to college without that experience, she may never have become as good a driver as she now is.

When Chris graduated from college, his Escort was worn out. I decided to get him one more vehicle for graduation. We chose a Toyota pick-up which he is still driving. Chris is now employed in Boise as a head hunter and doing well enough that he has invested in a used Porsche. He did not seek advice or money from me.

When I was a child, I never thought about needing to own or buy cars. Other children did, but they would be drivers. I knew I would be using public transportation or riding with other people. And for the first part of my adult life, that was true.

For the last 15 years, I have used my car regularly. I do not drive to work and never have. I now live about three-fourths of a mile from work and walk most days. When Laura comes to Boise, my car is available.

I did not teach my children to drive, but I played a part in the process. Since they lived with me, they heard what I had to say. I wanted them to be safe, considerate, and responsible drivers. When they were beginners, my presence in the car, doubtless, sometimes made a difference.

Buying that first van was an adventure, and I was not prepared for the disbelief that a blind person could want such a thing. But it was the beginning of more flexibility in my life, just as the first car is for most people. It gives me one more alternative for transportation.

In many ways cars in my family have been handled very much the same as in other families. Blindness adds a wrinkle, but it really doesn't change basic interactions. Will I continue to own a vehicle as long as I live? I cannot predict the future, but I have no plans to sell my Dodge. It is old, but I hope to get a few more years out of it. I'll cross the next bridge when the time comes.

A Hurried Exit

by Nancy Coffman

Nancy Coffman is an active member of the National Federation of the Blind. In her amusing account of a simple incident at a rest stop along a Nebraska highway, she reminds us that the conclusions we sometimes draw from what we see and which would seem to be obvious, are not always correct. Here is what she has to say:

I have been blind since birth, and many things have been said to me over the years which bring the fact that people have stereotyped expectations of blind people into my consciousness. My parents both worked hard to see that I grew up expecting myself to achieve and excel.

My mother's frustration with me as a child often led her to proclaim, "you think just because you are blind it's O.K. to. . . !" In my adult life, I came to realize that she and Dad, in their wisdom, wanted me to be aware of the stereotypes I would embrace and the self-fulfilling prophesies I would live out in my lifetime if I was not careful. She wanted me to be a competent adult rather than what the rest of the world would have molded me into.

As a blind person, I have sometimes found myself in situations where I honestly wondered if other people thought I had made a blunder because I am blind when in actuality, I had deliberately done what I did for a perfectly legitimate reason.

I often think of these situations and find humor in them knowing that if a sighted person had done what I did, no questions would have come to anyone's mind. One day, as my husband and I drove from our home in Lincoln, Nebraska, to Wyoming where both his family and mine lived, I had just such an occasion.

We had stopped at a rest stop about an hour from Lincoln to stretch and use the rest

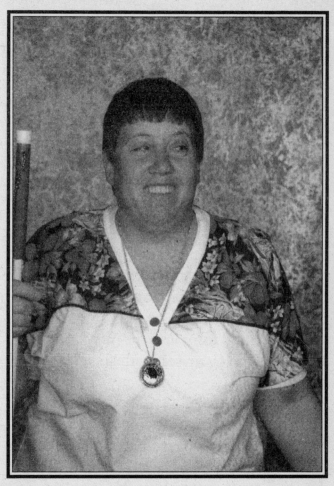

Nancy Coffman

room facilities. We often use rest stops when our schedule doesn't permit lengthy stops. One of us usually goes in at a time so as not to leave the car unattended. Taking turns also provides an extra minute to stretch, look at the map, or do other things that might need to be done.

On this occasion, my husband had come back to the car, and I headed in to use the rest room. Upon finding the women's rest room locked, I realized I had a decision to make. I could wait but that might mean making an extra stop, thus making our schedule even tighter, or, I could use the facility that remained open. I tugged at the other door and went into the men's rest room after announcing myself with "hello, anybody home."

All was well and the house was empty. I thought I had it made, so I proceeded. Before I could get myself prepared to leave, I heard the door open and close. Heavy footsteps echoed throughout the room. No stall doors closed, and nobody spoke. I hurried out behind the man who had come in behind me to use the urinal.

As I left quietly and quickly, I wondered what he thought. He had probably not checked the door to the women's rest room. He probably thought that my blindness caused me to enter the men's room in error. I smiled as I walked back to the car to find a giggling husband wondering the same thing.

We both knew that anyone who didn't know me would be persuaded by the age-old belief that sees blind people as incompetent. Surely that would be the only reason a blind person would show up in the wrong rest room. It made for great humor knowing that if he thought that, he was wrong. Blind people must do what they have to do just like everyone else.

BUT THE OTHERS
MAJORED IN MUSIC

by Hazel Staley

Hazel Staley served for many years as president of the National Federation of the Blind of North Carolina and at age 82 continues to be one of its principal leaders. Here she reflects on what it was like for a blind girl entering college in 1936. Hazel wanted to be a teacher, but in those days that was not to be. Hazel has worked for more than three decades helping to change what it means to be blind for those who are to come after her. This is what the National Federation of the Blind is all about. Here is what she has to say:

I lost my sight when I was two years old as a result of meningitis. I was number five in a line of six children brought up on a farm in Union County, North Carolina.

My parents sent me to the state school for the blind in Raleigh, some 200 miles away. It was not easy for them to send me so far away, but they knew I would need an education and that was the only place I could get one.

I finished high school with a fine record. I applied to and was accepted by Flora McDonald College. On registration day I took my place in line with the other freshmen. When it was my turn, I stepped up to the registrar's desk and gave her the preliminary information that she needed. Then she asked what degree I would be working toward. I said, "An A.B. degree."

She said, "Oh, Honey, I don't think you can do that. You see, it requires several hours of science lab, and you can't do that."

I said, "How do you know I can't? I haven't even had a chance to try."

She said, "We have had four other blind girls here, and they all majored in music. Why don't you do that?"

Hazel Staley

I said that I had had a lot of music in elementary and high school but that was just not what I wanted to do.

At this point the girl in line behind me stepped up and said, "Excuse me. We always work with partners in lab, and I'll be glad to be her partner. I don't think there will be a problem."

The registrar then said reluctantly, "Well— ah—I'll go ahead and put you down and— we'll see."

I hung around until the girl who had been behind me finished registering and walked out with her.

I said, "I appreciate what you did for me, but I can't help wondering why you did it, since you have never seen me before and don't know me."

She laughed and said, "I just liked the way you stood up for what you wanted, and I really don't see any problem. I believe that when a person spends money to come to college she ought to study what she wants and not what some stranger thinks she ought to do. That just doesn't make sense. You obviously have dealt with situations before and know what you can do."

The next morning someone knocked at my door and said that the dean wanted to see me in her office. I thought, "Oh, my! They're going to kick me out for being sassy. What will I tell Mama?"

When I walked into the dean's office she said, "We had a faculty meeting, and we have decided to put you on probation for the first quarter. If you do all right, you can go ahead with your A.B. degree."

I thought, "Probation indeed!" The only probation I knew about was what the court put bootleggers on down in Union County, where I was raised. My first impulse was to tell her that she could take her probation, her lab, her degrees, and the whole blankety-blank school and shove 'em. However, I realized that there was a lesson here that needed to be taught and that I was the person at the time and place to teach it. So aloud I said, "Thank you. I'll accept that."

Now I'm about as unscientific as anyone you're likely to meet, but my other subjects came easy. So I zeroed in on science. My friend was right. There wasn't a problem. At the end of the quarter I made the science honor roll and the dean's list. Four years later I received my A.B. degree.

I entered college in 1936 four years before the National Federation of the Blind was even organized, and it was more than thirty years later before I learned of its existence. But I knew instinctively that the registrar had no right to tell me what I could or couldn't do.

I had wanted desperately to teach high school English and French. I learned that in 1940, a blind teacher in a public high school from North Carolina was out of the question; so I turned to social work. I liked social work and was a good worker, but I gave it up in 1947, when I married. My husband was in military service, and I wanted to be free to go where he was.

In 1969 Federation leaders came to Charlotte to talk with us about organizing a chapter of the National Federation of the Blind. I was excited and delighted to learn that there were others who believed as I did. I knew that I had to be a part of this group. I became active in our local chapter immediately and went on to serve as state president.

At age 82 I'm still doing all that I can with the organization and will continue to do so as long as I live. I believe that the NFB is the greatest thing that has ever happened to blind people, and I'm proud to be a part of it. I want its work to continue for future generations of blind people.

To do what I can to make this happen, I have designated in my will a good portion of my estate to go to the Federation. My one regret is that they were not teaching mobility in North Carolina when I was growing up. This has been a real handicap to me. After I learned about the Federation I fought a real battle with our state agency for the blind to get mobility instructors in the state.

We still don't have enough instructors, but the agency's philosophy has changed for the better. I am thankful that in my own small way I have had the privilege of being a part of the National Federation of the Blind.

You can help us spread the word...

... about our Braille Readers Are Leaders contest for blind schoolchildren, a project which encourages blind children to achieve literacy through Braille.

... about our scholarships for deserving blind college students.

... about Job Opportunities for the Blind, a program that matches capable blind people with employers who need their skills.

... about where to turn for accurate information about blindness and the abilities of the blind.

Most importantly, you can help us by sharing what you've learned about blindness in these pages with your family and friends. If you know anyone who needs assistance with the problems of blindness, please write:

Marc Maurer, President
National Federation of the Blind
1800 Johnson Street, Suite 300
Baltimore, Maryland 21230-4998

WHY LARGE TYPE?

The type size used in this book is 14 point for two important reasons: One, because typesetting of 14 point or larger complies with federal standards for the printing of materials for visually impaired readers, and we want to show you what type size is helpful for people with limited sight.

The second reason is that many of our friends and supporters have asked us to print our paperback books in 14-point type so they too can easily read them. Many people with limited sight do not use Braille. We hope that by printing this book in a larger type than customary, many more people will be able to benefit from it.

Other Ways You Can Help the National Federation of the Blind

Write to us for tax-saving information on bequests and planned giving programs.

OR

Include the following language in your will:

"I give, devise, and bequeath unto National Federation of the Blind, 1800 Johnson Street, Suite 300, Baltimore, Maryland 21230, a District of Columbia nonprofit corporation, the sum of $_____ (or "___ percent of my net estate" or "The Following Stocks and bonds:_____") to be used for its worthy purposes on behalf of blind persons."

Your Contributions Are Tax Deductible